Unlegendary Heroes

Unlegendary Heroes

Mary O'Donnell

Salmon Poetry

Published in 1998 by
Salmon Publishing Ltd,
Cliffs of Moher, Co. Clare

A catalogue record for this book is available from the British Library.

Salmon Publishing gratefully acknowledges the
financial assistance of the Arts Council.

ISBN 1 897648 96 0 Softcover

Cover artwork by Austin Carey
Cover design by Brenda Dermody at Estresso
Set by Siobhán Hutson in Goudy
Printed by Betaprint, Clonshaugh, Dublin 17

Acknowledgements

Acknowledgements are due to the editors of the following publications in which some of these poems first appeared: *The Honest Ulsterman, Spark, Poetry Ireland Review, W.P. Journal, Acorn, The Irish Studies Review, The Seneca Review, The Literary Review* (NJ), *The Chariton Review, Crab Orchard Review, Lullwater Review, Barnabe Mountain Review, Solo* (CA), and *Tribuna* (Romania). Some poems were broadcast on RTE Radio and National Public Broadcasting (USA). The poem 'Bees and Saint Colman' was a prize-winner in the Austin Clarke Centenary Poetry Competition, 1996.

Contents

1.

In The Tuileries	3
One Sunday at Seapoint	5
French Fields	7
Mme Hoffmann's Lemon Tree	8
February Morning, California	9
Elder-Bush	10
Sleeping It Off	11
Bah Humbug	12
My Father Waving	14
Moon Over Monaghan	15
The Woman of the Lough	16
The Kilnadreen Cat	18
Heimat	20
A Southerner Dreams the Future	21
Unlegendary Heroes	22
The Two-Wheeler	25
The Cure	26
Bed-Time Stories	27
Her Sister's Bed	28
The Girl of 1960	29
Latin, 1963	30
45 Dublin Street	31
Materfamilias	32
This Child, This One	33
At the Zoological Gardens	35

An Island, One Winter   37

    Snow 1   37

    Snow 2   38

    Snow 3   40

Infant   41

Promise   42

Night Watch   43

2.

Talking to Mum Before Meeting Marie Stopes   49

Legend from the Far North   51

The Doll Factory   52

Kate O'Brien Weekender Meets

    La Leche Leaguers   55

Quartet   57

    Supermodel   57

    The Crouching Woman   58

    Camille Claudel   59

    La Grande Odalisque   60

A Private Life   61

Plath On Plath   62

Blue Velvet   64

10 Haikus on Love and Death   65

And Water Found Its Way   67

Bees and Saint Colman   68

Emilia Decorates Waterstown After
   the Death of her Son   70
Emilia, Crossing a Bridge, 1751   72
Emilia Mourns Her Son, 1764   73
The Bog-Witch's Daughter, One Summer 74
Giving Way   75

1

In The Tuileries

We misjudged the scale of things.
Two fifteen or thereabouts, we'd said.
Once off the *rue de Rivoli*, I knew
that we would wander without meeting.
I sat a while, back to the sun,
watched children send wooden sailboats
jagging at the ornamental pond,
hoped that you'd be drawn to those
who idled near the brittle floats.
An icy autumn day, lethal winds
in a high, blue sky drove fruits
and leaves to withdraw and sink deep.
No reference to a world rank
with injustice, no sense of all the wrongs
and all that stank about the universe.
Here, a place we'd read about,
a novelistic arena, a moment in a season,
where eternally, dogs and women breeze
by as if on wheels, and silent couples stroll
the yellowed grit between the trees,
and white-shod tourists like ourselves,
revisit all the chapters that they must.
We balanced as never before, but separately.
In all that vastness between us,
no exclaiming on symmetry or stone,
on sculpture or period; comfort for sure,
in a city endowed, but alone
with orangeries, trim trees in view,
the grand line of paths extended perspectives
beyond the usual limits. You felt it too,

I discovered later, and absence, as if
we'd inadvertently cleared the wrong fence,
then herded one another, prematurely, set to fail,
towards some final mortal innocence.
As so often, we misjudged the scale.

One Sunday at Seapoint

How transparent those crabs
In deathly buckets!
Children dare one another
Down the tide-tossed steps,
A child introduces herself

Over and over, then shrieks
At a maverick wave.
A light wind paws the rim of my hat.
In the bay,
Sails tug like hooks

Against Venetian blue.
Today, a different wildness in me,
Unleashed between snacks
Of ice-cream, crisps.
The children scream,

Possessed by comic djinns
Who hear a tornado,
Sense the centrifugal pull
As bones are driven against my skin.
The child who introduces herself

Over and over,
Runs past my moments of despair,
Arms flailing,
Voice rising in hilarity.
I lean forward on shingle

That grinds into panicking palms,
Bare heels.
Remember this, I whisper,
The teeth-like yachts,
Nibbling breeze,

Deft run of a retreating tide,
That original smell –
Kelp or brine –
When all the rest is forgotten,
Remember the child,

Crabs, minnows,
Children,
The transparency
Of imprint on any moment,
Those spectral watermarks.

French Fields

The first time I saw sunflowers
In a field, I knew the difference.

Our forced Irish ones,
Rain-shredded, spat on,
Limped in damp yellow
Towards an earwig-flecked harvest.

These French beauties had it all.
We pulled up on the road to Pau,
Stood in a field of yellow heads
That touched and tilted.

Magenta clay, tensile stems,
Those specked brown eyes –
A single dark depth of pupil
For every flower-head

Made love to by the sun.
They turned and turned
In a slow dance of yellow veils,
Acres and acres of simmering girls,

All eyes on the one man
They wanted to ravish
In mid-day fires,
A throb of cricket's wings.

Mme Hoffmann's Lemon Tree

The leaves shone,
Clustered around each poised lantern
As we sipped aperitifs
In a windless garden.

When Mme Hoffmann wasn't looking,
I let one lemon brush my hand,
Sensed the trembling, clear juices
Hugged within, an enviable tang.

My teeth went wet with the need
To bite, my eyes closed
At the prospect
Of colour, oil, acid.

I withdrew slowly,
Heard the sudden intake.
A whispered *Non, Madame!*
Pardon, I murmured,

as if the tree had spoken.

February Morning, California

Like garments trailing slowly
On the waiting ocean,
Those yellow, curdled fogs
Once quickened the pulse

Of Francis Drake's crew,
Set them thinking of limitless
Wealth as the prow of *The Golden Hinde*
Clove into thicketed bays.

Today, a week's dealing done,
Men walk dogs on wet marsh grass.
Nearby, the sea lumbers,
Invisible in the haze.

Away from Kinsale,
Aughrim or Killala, imprinted
With historical defeat,
I could have stayed,

Stretched out,
Safe
With what I could not see,
But merely sensed.

This morning,
The crest of Mount Tamalpais,
Once sacred to the natives,
Is under wraps.

Elder-Bush

A wedding.
A smell of lace,

fresh unpacked from
the dressmaker's box; my arms

are hung with creamy globes,
froth-notes that took a winter,

a spring, to sew.
When my lace

has worn itself to dark sacs,
and my fingers carry fruit,

the birds come,
probing me, finding juice

in the purple love-knots,
staining themselves

with the threads
of my death.

Sleeping It Off

Spring and summer
are hungover.

Insects and birds
made such a thing of growth.

The buzzing, pecking, biting,
have all but stopped.

I am on more than civil terms
with swallows heading south.

Crows shake the sky,
a cloth of oyster calico;

it wraps my ears with
winterish gossip.

Premature, of course.
The party's over.

I enjoy clearing-up
after visitors have gone.

The trees undress
to companionable nakedness.

Nothing expected
but silence.

Bah Humbug

Suppose, just when you'd left the tree to shrivel
     in the garden,
bagged the tinsel, rolled up the
     broken lights,
someone said 'Sorry folks, from now on
     it's Christmas all year round!'

Would you cope with the colour co-ordinated
     ribbons, the tartans
and pinks, the smell of resin, the unceasing
     entry and exit
of damp trees, the whole of Wicklow and Laois
     plundered for spruce?

And the dinners, greasy darning needles popping
     the loose flap
above the Pope's Nose, onion and butter
     beneath your nails,
and dinners and dinners, turkey, sprouts *a la Chinoise*
     festive and original,
the vegetarian sister, the brother who won't come
     because he's casting fairies in bronze
now that Christmas is forever, and the ones who must
     have home-made cranberry sauce or die,
the relentless flow of cards,
     from all of us to all of you, smiles across the miles,

and instead of Ian Dury
     The Pet Shop Boys U2 UB40, charity-boxes rattling,
rattling, carollers carolling forever,
     those gifts, those crackling gifts,

and the same kids on the streets,
    begging for a little help God bless ya ma'am
and may the little wan never want,
    and Christmas dole forever.

My Father Waving

In the New Year, we drove away.
I glanced back at the house on the hill.
It was shrinking, shrinking,
encased in ice, fragments of Christmas
in winking fairy-lights.
My father waved with both arms,
like Don Quixote's windmill.

On the brink of motherhood,
I saw lives swept almost to oblivion,
scuttled on reefs of the present;
then a processional, those quiet generations
moved through evening ice the colour of Asia,
described the entrances and exits –
parents of parents
like Russian dolls re-entering my body,
telling what was never told anyone,
announcing it now to my unborn girl.

The unstill past entered, forgotten
ghostlings and wanderers fussed
and made ready for the future –
one step ahead, bridging dawns,
afternoons between birthdays and Christmas.
The vision displaced the crammed wells
of fear, fed my courage.
In the New Year, we drove away.
The child turned beneath my ribs,
the parents of parents waved.

Moon Over Monaghan

A boy called Bartley turning my hair
in his hands as if it were sand;
we lurched uncertainly to *The Eagles*,
A Whiter Shade of Pale,
our fingers nervous as grenade-pins.
Everything was fear,
of skin, of lips, of speech.

Later, clouds gushed
on a millwheel moon,
that year, Apollo meant one thing only.
I would have preferred
Christmas cards with silver snow,
Victorian smiles,
to have been younger or older,
knowing Apollo meant light,
that the moon over Monaghan
had caressed shoals of fish,
the backs of elephants,
I would have preferred
to howl out loud
at an opal mirror in the sky.

The Woman of the Lough

People would talk about getting out
Of situations, or facing up to things,
About cute hoors or brave wee souls.
She always said perhaps, maybe,
We'll see how it works out.

But late one summer night, she went.
Few saw her wade in, or recognised
The yellow swimsuit, the red rubber hat
With half-perished daisies.
The water was like silk on her chest and arms,

That border lake smelt sweet
With secrets as she front-crawled
To the deeps they said were bottomless.
All those dawn swims amounted
To something, the frustrated pleasure

Of being on her own, an hour between
The panic of a teething baby
And the habit of a husband's face.
At least she got the swimming right.
Dipped duck-arsed, learnt to hold rage

As long as it took.
Deeper she went, further and deeper,
Across the silent lough,
Smiled to herself when she glimpsed
The bottom they said wasn't there.

Greenish brown, matted sludge,
Then patches of sand, the fish avoiding
Her. She was afraid of nothing.
The night she left, she dove beneath,
Emerged at the far side, newborn,

Slid into the waiting car.
By the time the boats came,
She was long gone.
Her swimsuit, her hat,
Floated in the dark.

Years later, she returned from Scotland.
People said she'd risen from the grave.
'And will y'stay?' her husband wondered.
'Perhaps. Maybe.
We'll see how it works out.'

The Kilnadreen Cat

He that dozed in my lap,
Soothing me with stillness,
Resolute sleep, a murmuring throat,
Lies stiff in the boot of the car,

Awaiting burial. John found him
In the wet summer grass,
Beneath a canopy of hogweed,
Near that bend where pines creak all year,

Where the stream in the bottom field
Wets the hill's ragwort mere.
He crossed the road,
Expended nine lives, his belly

Tight with summer mice and voles.
I phoned my daughter.
D-E-A-D, I spelt.
Tonight in bed, I'll see mint-green eyes

Blinking and darting, I'll feel
The pads of his paws as he spins
Through my fingers,
Teasing my hairless skin.

That teeming cat knowledge will stream out,
Away. He loaned all I ate and drank
In words and visions,
All blessings I was able to share,

The intelligence in every ray of light,
An inclination to curl close to the best,
Shunning cruelty, dour people, bores.
To my underworld he loaned his truth,

Restored now to his kind: over there,
Wildness is venerated more than youth.

Heimat

Kilnadreen was our patch,
south of Griggy, Drumgarn or Tirnaneill,
north of Coolshannagh, Tullyhirm, Kilnacloy.
Our hill, our fields, our stream.
The avenue buckled towards the outside world,
flinging dogwood and nettles,
docken leaves to cure a sting,
foxgloves, peonies, a neglected lily.
Summer after summer, *Philadelphus*
perfumed my white days.
In Kilnadreen, I learnt about peace,
how it thrived where soil was settled.
Kilnadreen was older than me.

Years later, when border 'copters hacked
the sky to shreds
over Griggy, Tirnaneill, Coolshannagh,
I saw my time, my youth, eclipsed
by hand-clasps and balaclavas,
by roaming lads who came to town
for the Saturday night disco.
The unbroken nerve of fag and whiskey breath,
boots and tartans,
those limbs like lances in the strobes,
the rapid flash of fingers,
battered my childish things,
leaving them for dead.
The cars retreated North,
roared across the hills,
then faded to a gnat's whine,
real and imagined.

A Southerner Dreams the Future

Gerry Adams at home.
His woman creating a mountainy haven
for the still-faced man.

Biergarten peace,
trellises and patio,
white-clothed tables.

Inside, the fruits of their loins
are tuning up on fiddles, mandolins.
Open windows face lakes and clouds,

winds are gentle, as if all
were resolved, as if all that remained
was aftermath, settling valleys,

tired memories. A dreaming heart,
almost deceived
by a hawk's solitary cry.

Not a blasted street, a shattered limb
in sight. Berchtesgaden 1996.
Sieg Heil!

Unlegendary Heroes

'Life passes through places.'
– P.J. Duffy, *Landscapes of South Ulster*

Patrick Farrell, of Lackagh, who was able to mow
    one acre and one rood Irish in a day.
Tom Gallagher, Cornamucklagh, could walk 50
    Irish miles in one day.
Patrick Mulligan, Cremartin, was a great oarsman.
Tommy Atkinson, Lismagunshin, was very good at
    highjumping – he could jump six feet high.
John Duffy, Corley, was able to dig half an Irish acre
    in one day.
Edward Monaghan, Annagh, who could stand on his
    head on a pint tumbler or on the rigging of a house.

> – 1938 folklore survey to record the local people
> who occupied the South Ulster parish landscape.

* * *

Kathleen McKenna, Annagola,
who was able to wash a week's sheets, shirts
    and swaddling, bake bread and clean the house
        all of a Monday.

Birdy McMahon, of Faulkland,
walked to Monaghan for a sack of flour two days before
    her eighth child was born.

Cepta Duffy, Glennan,
very good at sewing – embroidered a set of vestments
    in five days.

Mary McCabe, of Derrynashallog,
who cared for her husband's mother in dotage,
fed ten children,
the youngest still at the breast during hay-making.

Mary Conlon, Tullyree,
who wrote poems at night.

Assumpta Meehan, Tonygarvey,
saw many visions and was committed to the asylum.

Martha McGinn, of Emy,
who swam Cornamunden Lough in one hour and a quarter.

Marita McHugh, Foxhole,
whose sponge cakes won First Prize at Cloncaw Show.

Miss Harper, Corley,
female problems rarely ceased, pleasant in ill-health.

Patricia Curley, Corlatt,
whose joints ached and swelled though she was young,
who bore three children.

Dora Heuston, Strananny,
died in childbirth, aged 14 years,
last words 'Mammy, O Mammy!'

Rosie McCrudden, Aghabog,
noted for clean boots, winter or summer,
often beaten by her father.

Maggie Traynor, Donagh,
got no breakfasts, fed by the nuns, batch loaf with jam,
the best speller in the school.

Phyllis McCrudden, Knockaphubble,
who buried two husbands, reared five children
and farmed her own land.

Ann Moffett, of Enagh,
who taught people to read and did not charge.

The Two-Wheeler

Sadie's high black bike
Lay against the laurels
On the level stretch below the house.
Up and down I free-wheeled every day,
Left foot low enough to scuff the ground
If I wobbled.

The leather saddle
Nosed my back each time I jerked the brakes
In panic.
It took a week for me to raise that left foot
To the other pedal.
The wheels ticked, I slid through air,

Repeating, near disbelief,
This new completion.
My body sprouted wings,
I greeted air spirits like lost friends,
Gusted along the musky avenue,
Free and unafraid.

The Cure

Sadie's brother was a priest in Hong Kong.
The rest of the family lived
In a new two-storey house
With wooden sunbeams on the glass front-door.
Behind, the lime-sprayed homestead crumbled,
The nest that reared them used as a byre.
The brother wrote home regularly
About family matters, Irish friends.
Sadie knew nothing about Hong Kong,
Of antidotes for ancient ailments
Sold in incense-clouded rooms.
Her family found their own cure,
In a Mandarin exotic with concrete garden,
White walls, broad net-curtained panes,
The sun on the door
Always rising.

Bed-Time Stories

Phyllis told me
About haunted gateways,
Sheets of flame
In the branches of trees,
About hairy hands and cloven hooves.
She knew what happened in Hell,
How the Devil
Rammed a hot poker down your throat
When you asked for water.

Before a dance at *Swan Park*,
She became a pirouetting dream-doll
In a jet dress that fizzed with glamour,
The skirt plump with petticoats.
A slick of scented lipstick,
Blue eye-shadow, black liner,
She was all woman
Beneath a high stack of hair
Sprayed to Arctic solidity.

Out of Hell, the demon
who unromanced her lovely dress
with hairy, unwashed hands,
Courting in a web of gateway,
His body persistent in the car,
His winkle-pickered limb
Like a poker between her knees,
Stoking her, when all she wanted
Was a mineral at the dance.

My Sister's Bed

A month before giving birth,
I slept in my sister's bed,
in that childhood room
where we grew between sleep and light.
Under the slanting roof,
near an artery of chimney-breast,
I rested one last time
within the room's sheltering shape.

I saw again the propped dolls,
hurled shoes, discarded books.
Remembered feeling safe
in that shuddering house
during winter storms,
the plain happiness of spring dawns
when jackdaws courted on the roof.
A month before giving birth,
I slept there again.
The moon made music
in a bowed black sky
that held the world in its spin.

The Girl of 1960

When the crunch came,
her natural mother didn't want to meet.
A middle-aged woman
not much older than her daughter
would not greet her firstborn,
dared not unpick the well-darned tear
in a life uprooted in disgrace.

Now gentle, raging Margaret
sails the world in quest of mothers
who'll say *yes, you are good, you are
the best child ever, how I love you!*
She wants mothers –
great peacock's tails of them,
believing blood is thicker than water.

But one look
the other side of wise sayings,
plasma's as thin as H_2O,
and heart-bonds await her willing
entrapment. Perhaps in the end,
she must mother herself.
To her it comes sooner than to others.

Eventually, lost mothers
are found as found ones
are slipped loose
from the skin of generations.
Know that, raging Margaret,
lost gentle girl of 1960, know
all the mothers who think you are *good*.

Latin, 1963

A high bridge between lean cliffs of mornings,
an ascending stairway at evening
when incense trailed
across stained glass
the colour of apples, apricots.
The pattern of school days –
terraces of future marvels,
hints of bedazzlement in the glint
of a *gloria*, a blatant *adoremus*.

Mass was learnt in third class,
piled like enchanted gold
in the mind's bunker,
a section for every week until
we could respond to entire runs
of wide-vowelled spells.

Some habits take root through the tongue;
translation becomes automatic.
Something else too:
a gift to augment the spoken word,
to enter an hour, a life,
rigs and rushes of pleasure,
childhood's dilating toils,
the senses open to
adoremus, adoremus ...

45 Dublin Street

In the dream, I am back
in my grandmother's kitchen.
The range oozes
waves of porridgy heat,
stewed tea.
Newspapers are fanned
in an arm-deep window sill.
Outside, a clotted path
of saxifrage runs riot.
The walls are as then,
neutral emulsion
in an evening gloom.

Unlike then,
all is silent.
There are dream-props:
sofa, the long table,
a cut glass sugar-bowl,
that step into the sinister well
of a dark hall.

The symmetry of what is not,
what has been.
I remember.
Some nights I return
and sit, puzzled

by the silence,
and a grey spiral,
like flies, where human traces
still fizzle on the air.
Only the saxifrage grows.

Materfamilias

My grandmother had thirteen pregnancies,
Nine full-term. She, who came orphaned
At nineteen from Clogher to Monaghan,
Fell to undreamt streams of constant parenting:
Keeper of children's needs, keeper of spouse,
Two uncles, a doting, whispering grandmother.

In that tall-storied town house, place of
Darkened stairwell, high, mysterious attic gloom,
Beds with bolsters, a sunny, summer sitting-room,
She learned to rule an embattled roost,
Bartered away diphtheria, TB from her brood
Between two world wars and after.

A pansy-eyed flapper, she tended to herself
Obliquely, in astrakan, or snug suede shoes;
Ambitious for all, yet slow to praise for fear
Of spoiling with Hollywood notions, child-dreams,
Songs she herself was not allowed. Wintering ended
When grandchildren came along, and she grew mild.

By then, with two sons dead, she wore Queen Mother
Hats, like turquoise shells askance
On venerable hair. Would she do it all again,
My mother once asked. No chance, she said,
Womanhood, the struggle between self and others,
Was costly; to deal once with the rise and fall

Of life, of death, enough.

This Child, This One

A stake through the heart
impaling us to the counsel of flesh,
a command never again to be separate.

It is like winter,
which imagines withdrawal
from red, whirling days,
almost convinced of slumbering death.

All the time,
   stirrings.
Even in January, daffodil bulbs
split the earth's skin;
she is mottled and sensitive,
her slumber, a terrible dream
of what is seeding
and pervasive,
of pollens to come,
forbids flirtations
   of word or deed.

Our tongues set free
in an eternal spring,
   we babble,
test stems of consonants
between our teeth,

balloons of vowels tender
         in our mouths,
discern the salts, sugars,
that viscous glide
along the tongue's rim.

        So we live:
at the edge of spirit,
our hearts staked forever
to the grace of flesh.

At The Zoological Gardens

The smell is part of the reason I return.
    I have always come, alone, or with a lover,
Once newly-married, learnt early to avoid
    The Sunday empire of ice-cream and Coke.
Again, upwind, I catch the feline funk,
    A sullen whiff of cattish viscera,
All that is dispassionate and wild.
    Before the piebald Colobus Monkeys,
Buggy-pushing mothers point, explain.
    An Arctic wind is blowing now in May,
    But lonely lovers do not stay away.

Two hippopotami glisten in mud,
    Their grave, aquatic feet engulfed and slurping,
As if to siphon subterranean ales.
    Intent on exercise, I face the wind,
Scoot the buggy past a sombre couple,
    Past soignée Jaguars, (ignored by my child,
Who points a rhetorical finger at a sparrow).
    Again, all that is dispassionate and wild;
Downwind, I breathe the fug of warm cat flesh.
    An Arctic wind is blowing now in May,
    But lonely lovers do not stay away.

Punk madonna and infant, orangutans
    Embrace and snuggle deep; behind a grille,
A sociable black pig snorts: children shriek,
    Make retching sounds then speak of shit and filth.
Polar Bears slouch to the shape of bean-bags,
    Coal eyes senile, Sea Lions bask in a pool,

Bark and snigger at the trippers out from school.
Everywhere, the shivering shrubs, women
In anoraks; and now my child asleep.
An Arctic wind is blowing now in May,
But hungry lovers dare not stay away.

A topography of foulest primal moments,
(Reviled by thinking people in the know),
Nobody here on weekdays but natives
From a one-sexed continent, let loose
With others of the species. The women
Play Mummy, the children – vague, hysterical
Or sleeping, converge at last on a place
Of beautiful, wasted creatures,
Bored, their essences squandered for all time.
Lost forever to Arctic winds in May,
Lovers and loveless do not stay away.

An Island, One Winter

Snow 1

Like love,
born in an instant,
you think you know it
when branches shimmy into light.
It spreads to the soul,
you are taken, ravished
by an idea of intimacy.
Poised for more, then more,
it melts from your glance,
to nothing.
Look out.
The little firs, miserable
at shrinkage,
the loss of nerve.
Snow, love. Never enough.
The fleet earth, cowardly.

Snow 2

The silence of it.
When all the cries are muffled.
Infants. Women. A man alone in his mind,
his car inching down a blue glass motorway.
Lovers. Quenched footfall.
The silence
of a thousand years ago,
cattle shifting, cudding,
in the covered byre.

In snow, we learn distance:
the silence of neanderthals
shuddering in sleep,
survival through tallow,
rindered remains,
an ox tail charred in the flickering night.

After snow,
the hope of whiteness.
A threat of innocence secures us,
the future fizzles
outside the bedroom,
the house: the white roof,
the wings of dreams.

This silence is the future:
an invitation to those minutes
before survivors stir,
before the cries,
again, and again,
as fatal pollens
howl silently through skin.
Our assured legacy
after the trouble of living.

After infants, women,
after the lone men pacing
the dark of their lives.
After the lovers for whom
something was once unblemished,
hope like a branch in snow.

Snow 3

Almost the shortest day.
Sleet whistles to snow. The plum-tree
has claws, and the sundial smothers.
I once finished a novel on a day like this:
that evening in the city, people
deserted cars and walked. Written out
to the last full stop, I was happy to be swaddled
in the night's white chrysalis.

'Whassa?' you mutter now, peering
at the sky. 'That's snow' I say,
then write and re-write. Your hands pound
the damp panes, you are excited
by swags of bushes, the spiralling grey,
soft snow-stars fallen to earth.
Bored now, you crawl to the piano
and suck the peddles.

Soon you're at my knee, tapping,
patting, murmuring. One arm raised,
one finger points. Your eyes beckon.
When I point back, our fingers touch.
But we cannot beam pulses
drawn from sun on this short day,
we are not intimate enough
to tilt the planet southwards.

Minute by minute, we meet as strangers,
and I, the absent one, must explain.

Infant

for Martin and Anna

You perch in his arms
and gaze upon us from above,
an Infanta surveying minions.
Something about his strength
is different from mine;
you know it,
feel the full majesty of a good man's arms
sweep you serenely above trifles
like toys and rattles.
Up there, you discover perspective,
recreate for yourself the eyes of callers,
candid, unperturbed. You do not
smile until something is proven.
May the right man always kiss
and hold you.

Promise

I try not to cast too much shade.
Sin would be
to use the excuse
of her growth in my womb,
to imagine her as a limb of myself.
She is her own tree,
late-winter's indomitable shoot.
She takes cupfuls of sun.

I stand well clear
as the branches stretch,
like flutes playing allegros.
Not for anything
would I poison her
with an act of possession,
conceal her from the woodsman
whose task is to make room for all.

Night Watch

Up in this loft for the night,
I stand by a high wide window,
the futon spread, pillows thrown,
listen to our daughter's babble
as you read to her in the room below.

The stars are flung through invisible
webs above the estuary; tide is out,
shorebirds stab the gleaming residues,
probe silver flats, though it is late.
In the distance, the Hook lighthouse

sweeps this corner of the world,
carries across Bagenbun, to Bannow.
My eyes sail the space above trees,
estuary, link the moment
to the revolutions of stars,

conceits of light and distance.
I welcome this solid
drift from daylight rigging,
sleep will soothe the darkness in me
that struggles in glare:

with sleep, the long, slow dive
through the sea-green wall
that wrenches self from self,
with sleep, my finned, osmotic drift,
a thousand mermaid's welcomes.

Till then, I watch the known ocean,
resist my sunken self,
plagued with thoughts
of the submerged,
thoughts of the salvageable.

2

Talking To Mum Before
Meeting Marie Stopes

That night I phoned, late.
    I wanted to utter it aloud,
        something in my throat

about to slither towards your life,
    like the unformed thing it was,
        red, waxy yellow, a mistake

from the doll factory.
    I stopped of course.
        Your girl grown competent woman

slouched flat on her pillows,
    telephone tucked beneath her jaw,
        all easy mirth and a chuckle on her tongue.

I wanted to tell you
    of this journey, the next day,
        I wanted to pass my heart for safekeeping,

in case this moment
    made of me a doll among dolls.
        I wanted you to remind me

of a rough sweetness,
    the optimism of elder-flowers
        on a summer dawn,

some green excitement
in my years of running into life.
I have never been so grown-up, Mum.

I could not tell, even you.
When we hung up, I checked my holdall.
I dared not remember the infants.

Would have screamed, my mind
fixed on thundering glaciers
in those final hours.

On the wall, the indolent gaze of my Madonna,
that cerulean cloak,
the eyes of her remote child.

In another city, you slept.
Jets came and went, ripping the night,
stacked hours raided my blood.

I invested in darkness –
for my life, for asylum –
and preyed on your presence

that night in the world.

Legend from the Far North

She could not say why,
in those lost hours she healed herself
    of a ghost from Irish days.

By the shores of the Baltic,
she remembered a Northern prince
who made love to forests
when summer bent the trees
    to secrets in green.

Like a bog princess too long interred,
violated by blunt sunshine,
she sought the shelter of those trees,
    the heat of snow,
not love and not love-making.

In those days she waited
for her weak bleeding to halt,
to heal,
    did her best to think of
Christmas and reindeer, their
flying hooves crossing the stars,
velvet muzzles, plumes of frost,
the yellow bite of cloudberries,
and that dark, dark island,
where she could rest in a forest,
out of range of unwanted ghosts.

The Doll Factory

She is stepping out, see her stepping out today,
a Dublin dawn is imminent,
the departure lounge a place of snoozing civilities,
coffee and rolls,
an air of velvet brownness, man with briefcase,
the odd woman, very odd,
and her invisible doll, trailing the future,
balloons and ribbons.

The wind mizzles and slaps, 737s heave and wobble.
She has waited her whole life for a final adjustment,
announcing an indifferent universe,
arbitrary collisions in mid-air, in tunnels,
between cell and cell,
dawnings, not an aubade.

2.
Central European Time, Schiphol. Young men tinker
        with computer games,
the Duty-Free spangled with winking watches,
bottles of perfume and booze
like amber boats on their sides,
scent and ethyl alcohol,
the measurement of time, the relief of computers,
to help the doll people face the day.

A lone woman watches the man on the seat opposite,
he pretends to read the paper.
He wants to stare and stare, satisfy
a hankering for breasts and hair,
without intent.
Pretending to avert her gaze, she notes skyline,
brighter,
a thin lip, sugared lime crushed by rising sun,
a Tequila teasing her tongue, and salt
on the rim of a day where dolls and balloons trail.

3.
At Copenhagen, the sea has frozen.
   Ice licks
closer to the airport, an unfinished hem
on the snow-queen's gown;
in time, winter does its work, induces rest for the dolls,
    respite
from the clamour of porcelain and pewter,
the illusion of space
down the long aisles, the blonde efficiency
of dolls from the North, they could be
sixteen weeks, twenty weeks old,
suctioned clear in bowls,
threads of unravelled capillary.

4.
Over Dublin, the plane of the world tilts.
She is blinded
by the citrus rush of an indifferent sun,
freed from gravity,
sucked to the clouds, on her way to perform
the task.
Her doll is quite still.
    She is stepping out,
    see her stepping out today.

Kate O'Brien Weekender
Meets La Leche Leaguers

It was one of me to two of them,
all three of us livid and speechless
after catching the wrong train
at Limerick Junction,
finding ourselves back in that city
of eloquent streets.
We had to talk.
Their eyes were fervent,
their parkas like bronze shields
as they evangelised.
They showed me books, statistics,
proofs – the damning, unforgiveable
evidence that society's greatest joy
was to part a mother from her baby.

Then I got going,
my brain ablaze
after delivering a lecture
on The Writer as Storyteller,
oh I was ready, spread my texts,
proofs, the damning, unforgiveable
evidence that society's greatest joy
was to part a writer from her words.
'Look at Kate O'Brien!', I thundered,
'Banned! Banned! Banned!'
We sat up all night in the Gleneagle Hotel,
gorged chicken sandwiches and tea;
after, the whiskey,
then the phonecalls.

Anybody. Anywhere. A disgruntled couple
in the 044 area snarled at the La Lechers,
their bed-sheets rustling down the line;
some bloke in 065 breathed heavily
as I told him about my books,
groaned and then hung up.
The next morning we embarked on the correct train,
at the correct time, then parted,
our minds lucid, bearing
gifts we were unsure of,
from beyond the frontiers,
the bones of our lives suddenly exposed.
You could say a useful exchange
had taken place.

Quartet

Supermodel

My body is a reed,
a forked road,
bones mounted on
canvas.

My depths and extremities,
lured from their lair by
bolts of metered light –
viridian, indigo –
even the voice of a man in leather.
I play chameleon,
all parts negotiable.
Eyes change from blue
to brown,
neck lengthens
in the style of Ingres.
The tilt of a shoulder
invites all comers.

Clothed, I am a Japanese tree,
a maidenhair embrace,
leaning to what
the wind has taught.
I am all I dream of,
earn more than money,
a house in Monaco,
the love of a King's son.
I am first footprints of the future.
I arouse thoughts of death.

The Crouching Woman

Rodin, 1882, bronze, from The Gate of Hell, a commissioned
work part-inspired by Dante's Inferno, The Crouching Woman
was originally one of the crowd of the damned.

Writhing, not damned.
Waters broken before time,
caught in second-stage labour.
The rich, absorbed squat of her,
one shoulder sunk beneath open knees,
head inclined in concentration.
One hand clutches
a breast, the other is wrapped
around her ankles.
An invisible animal
mounts her back and shoulders,
grunts as it works
to open her up.
Her eyeballs roll
beneath closed lids,
she shudders on an out-breath.
Stuck at Hell's gate,
penetrated from within.
She moans for her father
through closed lips.

Camille Claudel*

I always knew what my hands could do,
listened to a master,
believed in his contempt for inspiration.
He'd thunder on about work, work, work.
Used my face once.
I became a limpid Aurora,
transparent as a snowdrop.
The most I ever shone.
I learnt my trade,
later, applied myself to art.
They barely waited till my back was turned,
sniggering at my diligence.
All the time I believed
in gods of marble,
so white they seemed hot,
I believed in tongues of fire,
in the mystery of hammer, chisel,
bronze and stone.
I became my own implement,
struggled in light or blackness,
no room for shadows.
Aged before time,
paraded myself in stinking garb,
to embarrass them,
my hair matted, my breath foul.
If even one had praised the work,
just one, I could have been saved.

*Camille Claudel, sculptor, was apprenticed to Auguste Rodin.

La Grande Odalisque
*after Jean Ingres**

Hours spread on a blue couch
that must not stain.
Beneath her, a swathe of cotton
to support her left hip.
He couldn't leave the neck,
the lumbar vertebrae alone,
wanted a sweep like a pulled, white bow.
Nothing wrong with that, he shrugged.
Her buttocks reached to her waist.

The room was airless.
They argued over the fly-whisk
and in the end she won.
Ochre feathers, beaded stem
displayed, delicate as a fan.
The brass orb made her think
of the Madonna.
Beneath the tasselled head-dress,
her serenest face
was alert to the sleeping child
across the room.
He smirked when she mentioned
the Holy Infant.

* The French neoclassicist Jean-August Ingres was renowned for
painting the female back as he felt it *should* be. Consequently, he
added vertebrae to provide the perfect elongation.

A Private Life

Flowers in the garden
go unnoticed,
Gold is spun in wasps' nests.
She is prepared
to push her hand in,
moves out at mealtimes.
During parties and farewells
for visiting ambassadors,
stillness laps at her work.
She gathers fragments for morning,
all the discards.
Her life is a mosaic,
pressed bit by bit
beneath the diplomatic clay.
Sometimes they dislodge soil,
almost connect.
In the end,
it's all imagination.
Even if they noticed,
she could not explain.

Plath On Plath
Sylvia Plath, 1932-1963

> *The possibility of accomplishing a creative act,*
> *of disclosing change and newness, is due to*
> *imperfection … That which reveals the image*
> *and likeness of the creator in man is the most*
> *imperfect thing in him, and is, it would appear,*
> *the outcome of imperfection, of incompleteness,*
> *of potentiality, of the presence of non-being within him.*
>
> – Nicholas Berdyaev

I had no time for it.
The matter of perfection
is central to the issue.
Who accepts defect
is no better than an idiot,
no better than my father,

eager to be beaten
by a colossus of transgression.
There was I,
my life, my children, my room.
But there was more.
People imagine that poets

burn and melt, giftless
beyond a stranglehold of words
that invades blood by osmosis.
Open my wardrobes then,
observe an excellence of image,
my suits, my swirling wools,

shoes built to tilt me
at just the angle
for the aesthetics of the pelvis;
once in Devon, in the pink-washed house,
my long floors, that bed,
my doorframes were for a woman's habitation.

As for non-being?
How they idle,
these fellows in search,
they pretend what is otherwise
somehow encompasses perfection.
Such criteria are good enough

for some men, most women,
for standard-bearers
of flawed light, the impure hour
between a briar of sex,
the rearing of children.
But not for me.

Something was intended.
Something else should have
happened. I could have made it,
were it not for poppies,
tulips, those prodding calyxes,
that well-loved male flesh,

poisoning my life.

Blue Velvet
To a fountain-pen

How the hand seeks balance
Between primitive thumb,
Rhetorical forefinger.
A gracious implement,
Blue and gold,
Her broad, tongued nib
Inscribed.
To write,
To stake a hinterland
On a black-tipped oracle.
Each word reflecting light,
Plays with letters, like a mirror
On a telescope, seizes past years.

The resting eye
Enchanted by filaments of black light,
Coils of syntax like unfolding nebulae.
Through it all she balances,
A sheath of blue velvet,
Contained, rippling
Within maidenly gold bands.

10 Haikus On Love And Death

1.
The man in winter.
His body is a warm cave.
Feel the low fires burn.

2.
Fingers in the soil.
The silent knowledge of roots.
From darkness to light.

3.
They speak of rising.
From what can we rise but death?
Now for the living.

4.
Dog of the spring night,
A frieze of leaves in moonlight,
Frost glitters on fields.

5.
My love's bright flower.
His leaves in a sheen of dew.
His passionate root!

6.
The girls swim like fish.
Hither in the deft ocean.
Minnows seeking warmth.

7.
And if I die now,
Will what is done be enough?
Winter is my judge.

8.
Foxgloves at twilight,
Dipping with purple secrets,
Mauve sheaths drip pollen.

9.
Woman in August.
Her body is a forest.
Here there is welcome.

10.
The red lips of June,
Shirts of sun, ribbons of moon,
How radiant is love!

And Water Found Its Way

Into my life, the white knights
rode around and around,
their stallions quivered,
froth from the leering velvet muzzles.

Those black horses screamed,
nostrils white with the riders' fear and fury.
They circled tents that no longer existed,
could not forget Karelia, Karelia:
but into my life, a murmuring stream.

Bees And Saint Colman

There was one who loved,
watched and handled us

when others feared the hives.
One night as he slept,

a chalice was stolen.
The saint wept for the loss

of the cup of Christ's passion.
We pitied him,

flew to dance a map,
the better that each should tap

the ripest clover,
spotted foxgloves, heather beds

until our sacs were swollen
with a high summer's fill.

Prayer withered his anger;
he almost forgot the sin of theft.

A morning came when,
entering the oratory,

he beheld a newmade waxen form,
a gold-combed, burnished stem,

wrought from our diligence.
He fell to his knees as if bereft.

Again we pitied him,
for his God, his silence,

those indolent prayers that forgot
the passion of our pollen.

Emilia Decorates Waterstown
After The Death of Her Son*

There are places for comfort in death.
This is mine.
Go, lackeys, skivvies,
muck-skirted girls
from the hovels of Maynooth,
go home to your broths and breads.

Leave me this – Waterstown –
a cottage for his jest, his play.
These shells I here lay
are the boats of his dreams,
that pearled trail,
oyster like magicked wings,

fantail-festoons of eggs in windows,
quartz and coral
from deeps of earth and sea
entice him to peep here and play
beneath the moonlit cupola.
Marbles and baubles await him.

If I sit in one corner,
behind the threads of a fine marriage,
he will not mind.
If I sit to one side,
playing cards, he'll remember
the half of me, quietly wild,

awaiting some return
in the annex
of my husband's estate;
the other, card-playing half,
loaded and loud
with grief's dice.

*Emilia Mary, daughter of the Duke and Duchess of
Richmond, married James Duke of Leinster in 1747
and went to live at Carton in Kildare. She supervised
the alteration of an old thatched cottage called
Waterstown into a shell cottage. It is thought that
one wall may have been ornamented by Emilia herself,
after the death of her son.

Emilia, Crossing A Bridge, 1751

That evening in autumn,
I gathered my own season,
remember a house flushed with sun,
the bridge over the Rye in spate,
carriage-wheels grinding between
the narrow trees.
I sensed my own slippage,
a life hooped and crammed
in the middle-distance
of history.

It fell on me like a cowl;
recognition of an ending
in coppery falls and silent trees,
in the wide, white immensity of my home.
I crossed the river, gathered myself,
clapped my hands,
drove black horses towards the late sun.

Emilia Mourns Her Son, 1764

For now, avoid the moon,
secretive woods,

the low lake of Donadea,
avoid any place of chimera,

where mists conspire with doubts
and dreams. If I imagine him there,

I will turn away, if golden light
entrances, I'll veil my eyes,

shutter my soul against
wet summer dews, stop ears, eyes,

allow nothing to enter,
glide, be smelt or tasted,

forget sights of darting wrens,
beech-trees shimmering at dusk,

nothing loved, nothing flaunted
by nature, no passionate act must stir

to hope. Rest will not come,
rest eludes as it has always done.

The Bog-Witch's Daughter,
One Summer

My threadwork spread out and dyed,
Abandoned on gardens and fields,
The ripples, tucks, lime-berries
In snoods beneath canopies of leaves.

A hiss of dry grass, blown kiss fairy-horns,
Armfuls of birch, bend, drape, rustle;
Cooking apples like green roses at dusk.
Flat on the plain, I gorge my lungs
On heather perfume, earth-musk.

If my child were dead,
None of that would matter,
No flags of colour, no spell,
Friend, foe nor life itself,
Would make summer ring my heart's grim bell.

As summer is, so my child –
Babe bog-witch, Irish primitive,
Fierce white seed, lost to reason,
Summer carillons mark her season.

Giving Way

The last journey takes place
in a train.

There is no rain,
only dawn rising outside the windows.

Towards the very end, the train slows,
drawing us gently through that final

thicket, banks stacked with primroses,
gorse in bloom,

casual reminders of how we lived.
In those moments when wheels and track

sing their harmonies,
we hold our breaths, watch

for the banked green bushes,
May flowers to gather in at last.